Original title:
The Coral Reef's Song

Copyright © 2025 Creative Arts Management OÜ
All rights reserved.

Author: William Hawthorne
ISBN HARDBACK: 978-1-80581-634-8
ISBN PAPERBACK: 978-1-80581-161-9
ISBN EBOOK: 978-1-80581-634-8

Tales Spun in the Current's Embrace

Beneath the waves, the fish all dance,
In silly hats, they take a stance.
A crab in a tux, quite the sight,
Twirls with a clam, oh what delight!

An octopus with eight left feet,
Trips on a shoal, it's quite the feat.
A dolphin plays hopscotch on the sand,
While jellyfish wave their tentacles grand!

Seahorse prances with utmost grace,
Shoaling shrimp join in the race.
A parrotfish hums a goofy tune,
While sea cucumbers sleep 'neath the moon.

With bubbles bursting, laughter roars,
A mermaid swoops by, shouting 'More!'
In the colors of coral, antics unfold,
In this underwater world, bright and bold.

Enchanted Garden of Marine Life

In the sea, a dance so bright,
Bubbles floating, pure delight.
Fish in tuxedos, swim and twirl,
Crabs in top hats, give a whirl.

Anemones wave, a jolly cheer,
Jellyfish giggle, with no fear.
Starfish clapping, a round of applause,
Octopus juggling, just because!

Poetry of the Plankton

Tiny critters in the blue,
Writing sonnets that are new.
With each swirl, they spin a tale,
Riding waves like a tiny whale.

Floating freely, they do a jig,
Dancing light, oh how they gig!
Sprinkling sparkles, they sing along,
In their world, they feel so strong!

The Ocean's Gentle Whispers

Whispers of the waves, so sweet,
"Hey there, fish! Come dance on your feet!"
Seahorses sway like they're at a ball,
While seaweed does the limbo, standing tall.

Crabs chirping jokes, they can't resist,
A game of tag with a flick of a mist.
Don't mind the sharks, they've lost their way,
Bumping into rocks, they're here to play!

Castles of Life in the Blue

In castles made of coral delight,
Sea turtles waltz in the soft moonlight.
Clownfish laughing, oh what a scene,
Playing tag with a sea cucumber queen.

Eels with wigs, stylish and bright,
Pose for selfies, what a sight!
With laughter echoing, a joyful tune,
In the kingdom beneath the silvery moon.

Colors of the Submerged Symphony

Bubble-blowing fish take a leap,
In a waltz with a crab, oh what a sweep!
An octopus juggles with style and flair,
While the clownfish giggles, with bright orange hair.

Seaweed dances to its own tune,
As turtles glide under the silver moon.
A starfish tries to do a pirouette,
But trips on a clam, you bet, you bet!

Chants of the Ocean's Heart

The sea slugs sing in a bizarre choir,
Making tunes that no one can aspire.
A jellyfish wiggles with a bright pink glow,
And sea horses prance like they steal the show!

A dolphin grins with a splashy cheer,
While seashells gossip; oh dear, my dear!
The waves crash in with a comedic clout,
As laughter spills from the deep; no doubt!

Murmurs from Beneath the Surface

The pufferfish blows up with a huff,
Saying 'Look at me, I'm really tough!'
A shrimp slips on seaweed, whoosh, he goes,
While a grouchy old grouper just strikes a pose.

Coral giggles in colors so bright,
While anemones wave 'hey, what a sight!'
An eel cracks jokes with a slithering charm,
Spreading laughter, spreading warmth, doing no harm.

Celestial Choir of Reef Life

Tiny fish gather, it's time for a show,
With synchronized swimming, they dazzle below.
A hermit crab tap dances on a shell,
While seahorses twirl, oh what a swell!

The barnacle band plays a catchy beat,
As the ocean floor shakes beneath their feet.
With a flick of a fin, all join in the fun,
Underwater antics for everyone!

Tales from the Tide Pools

In tide pools wide, where crabs like to dance,
Starfish spin tales, given half a chance.
Sea snails in hats, they party all night,
Throwing shell confetti, such a dazzling sight.

Tiny fish gossip, in bubbles they speak,
Their secrets are silly, but oh so unique.
With wiggles and giggles, they share their small schemes,

Making waves of laughter, like wild, playful dreams.

Melodies of the Fish Folk

The fish folk gather, holding finned soirées,
With seaweed streamers and many fishy plays.
They sing silly verses in bubbles of mirth,
Creating a chorus that rocks the sea's hearth.

Their scales all glitter, a colorful sight,
As they shimmy and shake, what a joyous delight!
With tales of lost boots and the clams' funny quirks,
Even octopi giggle with their ticklish works.

The Secrets of Sea Anemones

Oh, sea anemones, so jolly and bright,
They wave at the fishes, like kids in pure light.
With tendrils that tickle, they laugh with pure glee,
Playing hide-and-seek with the sprightly young sea.

They occasionally squabble, "That's my coral chair!"
Then back to their games, without a single care.
Their jokes are quite buoyant, they float and they dive,
In the chaos of colors, they really come alive.

Shimmering Voices in the Deep

Beneath the blue waves, where the wonders reside,
Lies a chorus of voices, too bubbly to hide.
"Hey there, my buddy, let's swim in a line!"
"Watch out for that rock, it's a slippery pine!"

With dolphins that giggle, and sea turtles sigh,
They frolic and flip, as the currents float by.
Their humor is timeless, it echoes through time,
With a rhythm of laughter, matching the rhyme.

Whispers Beneath the Waves

Fish in funny hats swim by,
Telling tales as bubbles fly.
Seahorses dance, quite out of style,
With their goofy grins, they beguile.

Crabs doing the cha-cha with flair,
While jellyfish float without a care.
An octopus tries to juggle fish,
But slips and falls—oh, what a wish!

Starfish playing cards on the sand,
Cheaters, too, with a finny hand.
A clam sings loud, thinks it's a star,
But only the shrimp know who they are.

In this wacky world beneath the tide,
Underwater laughter, our playful guide.
The ocean's secrets in giddy spins,
Where everyone's lost in silly grins.

Tides of Color and Light

Rainbow fish wear polka dots,
Swimming by in quirky knots.
Clownfish giggle, making a fuss,
While sea turtles ride the bus.

A school of fish holds a talent show,
With a starfish crooning—oh what a blow!
Corals blush in hues so bright,
As they sway to the marine delight.

The seaweed wiggles, a playful dancer,
A crab in a tux—what a romancer!
Every wave bursts into laughter,
As sunlight glimmers, ever after.

Underwater joy, a vibrant scene,
With silly moves from the fishy team.
The tides of color, a cheerful sight,
In this realm of fun, pure delight.

Symphony of the Sea

A conch shell plays its silly tune,
While dolphins twirl beneath the moon.
Clams clash cymbals, oh what a sound,
While sea cucumbers groove around.

The bubbles pop like tiny drums,
As fish dance in electric jumps.
Anemones sway, with arms stretched wide,
In this sea symphony, we take pride.

A blue whale hums a bass line deep,
While squids create art in a leap.
Turtles clap in their slow-motion,
Echoing joy with every ocean.

So join the fun, let your heart soar,
In this underwater concert, forevermore.
With every splash, a giggle and cheer,
The symphony of the sea brings us near.

Echoes in the Deep

Whale songs echo, funny and grand,
As fish giggle in a merry band.
An eel whispers jokes, quite absurd,
While crabs clap claws—how very heard!

In the depths where silliness reigns,
A sea urchin plays its spiky games.
Octopuses twirl in a dizzy display,
While mermaids laugh the day away.

Pufferfish puff, but not from fright,
Throwing bubbles that twinkle in light.
A catfish sneezes—oh, what a sound!
As everyone joins in, joy is found.

In the echoes where laughter swims free,
We'll dance together, just you and me.
With every wave, a chuckle or cheer,
In this playful world, forever here.

Lullaby of the Ocean Floor

In a sea where the fishes giggle,
A crab tries to dance, but he wiggles.
An octopus plays peek-a-boo,
With shells that hide treasures anew.

Starfish wear hats that don't quite fit,
While sea turtles take naps—what a hit!
They snore in sweet harmony,
Under waves, so carefree and free.

Clownfish paint stripes for a show,
While jellyfish float with a glow.
Seahorses prance with a twist,
Creating an underwater tryst.

So come dive in, bring your cheer,
For the ocean's laughter is always near.
Each splash brings a giggle and a glee,
Let's join in this song, wild and free!

Melodies in the Tide's Embrace

A dolphin leaps, slips, and spins,
While seaweed sways, with its quirky grin.
Anemones bounce in a silly jig,
As fish swim by, oh so big!

With clowny faces, the pufferfish pout,
In bubbles of laughter, they twist about.
Shrimps throw a party, where they sashay,
And starfish cheer from a rock ballet.

Mollusks play music with their shells,
In a symphony where laughter dwells.
The tide sings a ditty, light and sweet,
As crabs chase their tails to the beat!

So dance along where the currents swirl,
In the melody where sea life twirls.
With joy in the depths, let the fun unfold,
In waters where tales of laughter are told!

Chorus of the Multicolored Depths

Bubbles pop with a giggly tune,
As fish swirl around like a cartoon.
Coral castles are buzzing with cheer,
In every nook, there's laughter here.

A grouper grins, he can't help but grin,
With his pals joining, it's a silly win.
Blowfish puff up for a tickle fight,
In the shimmer of day, all feels just right.

The sea cucumbers shimmy and sway,
To sing of the joy in a whimsical way.
Each wave brings a chuckle, a splash of fun,
In depths where the humor has just begun.

So gather the friends, come join the spree,
In the colorful depths, so wild and free.
With giggles and wiggles, the ocean sings,
Creating the happiness that laughter brings!

Symphony of the Sunlit Lagoon

In a lagoon where the sunlight beams,
Colorful fish swim in cartoon dreams.
A turtle rides waves with a goofy grin,
As laughter bubbles up from within.

Giggling starfish spin with flair,
While sea otters splash without a care.
Crabs tap dance on shells all around,
Creating a beat with a silly sound.

Each sea urchin jives with a waddle,
As clams clams up for a light-hearted model.
The waves join in with a playful rush,
In this watery haven, we all want to hush.

So come take a dive, and don't forget,
The lagoon's a wonder, full of jest.
Where every ripple is a tale to tell,
In the sunshine, where laughter dwells!

Whirls of Life in Aqua Dreams

Bubbles dance like little clowns,
Fish in tuxedos swim upside down.
Seaweed sways, the laughter grows,
Turtles race as everyone knows.

Octopuses juggle with great flair,
Starfish gossip without a care.
Crabs doing salsa, can't miss a beat,
While seahorses strut in tiny feet.

Dolphins play tag in crystal blue,
A wise old grouper gives a view.
Waves clap hands, the ocean plays,
In this wild world, fun never strays.

Vibrant Voice of the Undersea Realm

A clownfish jokes with a punchline bright,
As dolphins giggle with pure delight.
Sea cucumbers lounge, unimpressed,
While jellyfish float in a glittery dress.

Eels tell tales of their wiggly might,
In burrows and crevices, hides young fright.
Mussels hum tunes, a shellfish band,
All join in a quirky, aquatic land.

Frogs in tuxes leap with a grin,
Shrimps tap dance, let the fun begin!
Colorful fish create a parade,
As laughter echoes in oceanic shade.

Serenading Shadows among the Anemones

In the shadows, a wink and a wink,
Where tiny shrimp and fish love to sync.
Anemones sway, a whimsical dance,
Offering sea stars a chance to prance.

Gobies gossip, with stories grand,
About the day's latest beachy band.
Tangs wear crowns of kelp and glee,
As otters share tales of mischief, you see.

Waves whistle tunes in a coral choir,
Tickling kelp with a giggly fire.
The ocean chuckles, shadows alive,
Together they sing—oh, how they thrive!

Destiny Woven in Coral Threads

Coral castles, with turrets of glee,
Baking under the sun, who could disagree?
Clownfish camp, plotting their next prank,
While parrotfish graze, not a thought to tank.

Lobsters arm wrestle in the sand,
An army of seahorses taking a stand.
A crab lifts weights, with muscles so strong,
Sharing a jest about where they belong.

In this kingdom where silliness reigns,
Frogs croon tunes in their underwater lanes.
The joy of this world, a bright, silly thread,
In the heart of the ocean, where laughter is spread.

Rhythms of the Briny Deep

In waters where the fish all dance,
A clownfish wears a polka pants.
The turtles glide, so slow and sly,
While starfish cheer, they yell, "Oh my!"

The seaweed sways with a giggle and glee,
As jellyfish float like they're sipping tea.
A crab in a hat offers jokes galore,
While octopuses juggle, we all beg for more.

A dolphin laughs with a bubbly tune,
While seahorses twirl like a cartoon.
The rhythm of tides keeps the beat in play,
Where every wave holds a joke to say.

So join the dance in the salty spree,
Where laughter and bubbles merge joyfully.
In this shimmering world, you'll never feel down,
With jests of the ocean, we're all cast in clown.

Secrets of the Coral Carnival

Beneath the waves where colors flash,
Anemones wiggle in a bright, wild clash.
Clams wear their shells with a proud little strut,
While fish play tricks, like a well-rehearsed cut.

A shrimp in a tux shows off his slick moves,
While parrotfish groove to the underwater grooves.
They've set up a party, you should come see,
With coral confetti scattered wide and free.

The sea cucumbers roll in with a cheer,
Singing old sea shanties for everyone near.
The bubbles are popping like fireworks bright,
In this carnival, everything feels just right.

So grab a shell phone, let's call all our pals,
Invite the sea stars, the sea urchin gals.
Together we'll frolic till the sun starts to set,
In a world full of secrets, we'll never forget.

Rhythm of the Underwater Bloom

In gardens deep, where the sea fans flourish,
The clownfish tell tales of who goes and who's nourished.

Little shrimp with their tiny top hats,
Act out whole dramas that might make you laugh.

The corals are giggling, in colors alive,
As snails trot by with their slow, silly drive.
Tropical fish make a splendid parade,
Each one with a sparkle, they're never afraid.

An octopus pops out with a wink and a grin,
While sea urchins chuckle, "Hey, let's dive in!"
A school of bright fish creates quite a scene,
In this world of merriment, where nothing is mean.

So dance through the bubbles, enjoy the excuses,
In the blossoms of ocean, make friends, spread your muses.
The rhythm of laughter unfolds all around,
In this underwater bloom, joy truly is found.

Tales from the Fathomless Blues

Down in the depths, where the goofballs play,
An eel tells a story in a wiggly way.
The clownfish chuckle, tails all a-flick,
While sea cucumbers dance to the beat, oh so quick.

With bubbles as notes, the sea sings a tune,
As crabs start a conga beneath the bright moon.
A narwhal pops up with a trumpet in tow,
And off they all go in this whimsical show.

A seahorse juggles kelp with brilliant flair,
While flounders stay flat, pretending not to care.
But every fish knows, from the big to the small,
That deep down in the blues, laughter conquers all.

So gather your pals for a deep-sea ballet,
In this fathomless world where fun leads the way.
The tales are outlandish, the humor is grand,
In the ocean's embrace, let's dance hand in hand.

Colors Between the Tides

Fish wear suits of vibrant hue,
Seaweed dances, what a view!
Crabs in hats that wobble and sway,
Even the starfish has something to say!

Seashells gossip, gossip they do,
Turtles wear sunglasses, oh so cool!
The sea cucumbers giggle in glee,
Making jokes with the anemone!

Brightly striped and polka-dotted,
Bubbles burst, and laughter's spotted.
Jellyfish jiggle, oh what a sight,
Underwater parties, pure delight!

So dive right in, don't be shy,
Join the marine fun, give it a try!
Under the waves, joy flows like rhyme,
In the ocean's depths, we laugh on time!

A Canvas of Life in the Abyss

Colors swirl like paint on a sheet,
Clownfish dance, how silly their feet!
An octopus juggles shells with glee,
While seahorses twirl, oh can't you see?

Nemo wears stripes, it's quite the trend,
While eels do yoga around the bend.
Urchins giggle, spiky yet sweet,
Making faces, oh what a treat!

Tropical hues in a splashy parade,
A pufferfish struts, sporting his shade.
The conch shell sings a tuneful joke,
As hammerheads spin, oh what a poke!

Together they paint with colors so bright,
Life's canvas alive, a marvelous sight.
In oceanic laughter, we find our bliss,
And dance through the depths, we cannot miss!

The Melancholy of Coral Reefs

A clownfish sighed, oh where's the flair?
His coral castle's lost its care.
With waves like whispers, troubles arise,
As barnacles frown beneath dreary skies.

Anemones hang their heads in despair,
While turtles reminisce of a time more rare.
Seashells look on, their colors fade,
Even sea urchins wish for a parade!

The blues of the ocean have turned to gray,
Where once was laughter, now silence weighs.
But wait! A spark, a tickle of light,
A school of fish breaks the gloom with delight!

Bright fins, new tunes, and joy on the rise,
Coral takes heart, lifts its head to the skies.
For under the surface, life still grooves,
And laughter returns in playful moves!

Coral Crystals Beneath the Surface

Under the waves, where the giggles reside,
Coral crystals shine, oh what a ride!
A mermaid plays tunes on a bubble-filled flute,
While fish join the chorus, oh how they scoot!

A clam claps its shell to the rhythm so sweet,
As dolphins spin 'round, oh what a feat!
Eels do the worm, such funny old tricks,
Spinning and swirling, a sea life mix!

In cracks and in crevices, laughter will bloom,
As colorful wonders consume the gloom.
Starfish chuckle, their limbs all a-flare,
With smiles so bright, they float without care!

So splash through the depths, join the grand fun,
Where joy is abundant and laughter's on the run.
Across coral crystals, let's dance and sing,
In the ocean's embrace, we'll find everything!

Ode to the Anemone's Dance

In the sway of currents they laugh,
Bobbing like clowns, a silly gaffe.
Tentacles wave in a joyful spree,
Inviting fish to join their jamboree.

Oh, what a jig under the sea's light!
Fishy friends twirl, oh, what a sight!
Anemones grin, waving like stars,
Who knew a sea anemone could go this far?

With bubbles bursting, they spin and twirl,
Making waves in an underwater whirl.
Their playful giggles, a watery cheer,
Turn serious sharks into a wiggly dear!

So here's to the dance, so wild and free,
Where even the frowniest creatures agree.
In the laughter of the ocean's embrace,
Life's jokers unite in this wondrous place!

Vibrations of a Subaquatic Dream

Air bubbles hum a jazzy tune,
Fish jive along, under the moon.
Coral critters strum their shells,
Creating a rhythm that chimes and dwells.

With a flip and a flop, they go in sync,
Dancing to vibes before you can blink.
Starfish claps on their five sandy hands,
While sea cucumbers form rock bands.

Jellyfish flail with a ghostly grace,
Making the seahorses join the race.
Laughter bubbles up from the tides,
In this ball of blue, where humor abides!

Tune in the waves, they tell a tale,
Of underwater antics that never pale.
So when you're down, sing like a fish,
And let your dreams swim, that's the wish!

Twinkles in the Corals' embrace

Coral castles glimmer and shine,
Where fishy actors perform in line.
With a wink and a swish, they take the stage,
Creating a show that's all the rage!

Clownfish giggle in bright orange hues,
While parrotfish boast of their colorful views.
An octopus juggles shells with flair,
While all of the sea life stops and stares.

The sea cucumbers tumble and roll,
In a funny ballet that steals the show.
Barnacles cheer from their rocky seats,
This curtain call brought aquatic beats!

In this underwater circus of fun,
Every fish laughs, oh, what a run!
So here's to the twinkles in aquatic dreams,
Where laughter bubbles like sun-kissed streams!

The Aquatic Waltz

In the sea's grand hall, creatures prance,
With nimble fins, they start to dance.
The krill pass by in a wobbly line,
While shrimps tap-tap in a rhythm divine.

A jellyfish floats in a shimmering gown,
As angelfish twirl, crab for a crown.
With a splash and a giggle, they whirl about,
Turning the ocean into a joyful shout.

Watch out for the clumsy sea urchins, too,
Who tumble and roll—it's quite the view!
The sea turtles glide with effortless grace,
All joining in for a fin-flapping race.

And though some may trip on the kelp's snare,
Everyone laughs; oh, truly rare!
In the rhythmic sway of the ocean's call,
Life's a dance floor, where all have a ball!

Beneath the Surface Lyric

Bubbles rise, fish giggle loud,
A crab performs, he's quite the crowd.
Seaweed dances, sways to beat,
A watery disco, oh what a treat!

Starfish spin in a twisted dance,
While clownfish joke, they take a chance.
They slip and slide on slickened stone,
Under the waves, they throw a bone!

Octopus boasts, with eight-armed flair,
His buddies cheer, they really care.
They throw a party, narwhals attend,
With laughter echoing, around the bend!

In this bright world of laughter's glee,
Even the angler's fish grins with glee.
They croon and croak, 'til the sun goes down,
Each fin and scale wearing a crown.

The Palettes of Aquatic Artistry

Splashing colors everywhere,
A painter fish, with brilliant flair.
They dip their fins in coral hues,
Creating scenes that one can't refuse!

Seahorse prances in hues of gold,
His art form? Well, it's never old.
With barnacles as stylish hats,
They laugh and boast, like cool old chaps!

Tropical fish in rainbow suits,
Strutting like they own the roots.
A jellyfish's wobbly wisp,
Makes all the critters take a lisp!

Brushes made from seagrass green,
Drawings made in the ocean sheen.
With joyful splashes in the sea,
Artistry reigns, wild and free!

Underwater Whispers

Whispers float on currents light,
Octopuses gossip, all through the night.
A turtle chuckles, spinning tales,
Of daring deeds and swimming fails!

Clownfish giggle, in sneaky tones,
Tickling each other with funny jones.
They spin around in coral caves,
Sharing secrets of ocean waves!

Shrimps are busy, making plans,
While sea cucumbers dance in clans.
They whisper softly, 'What a show!'
As dolphins flip, with grace they flow!

The murmurings rise like swells at sea,
Echoing fun, where all are free.
In this world where giggles launch,
Underwater friends share a staunch!

The Fabled Colors of the Brine

Fabled hues of blue and green,
All the vibrant shades between.
Fish parade with flashy fins,
Joking 'round like goofy twins!

Anemones tickle little toes,
With gentle sways, they steal the shows.
While wrasses wave with sassy glee,
Making jokes about the sea!

Corals blush in hues so bright,
Dancing in the warm sunlight.
With laughter echoing all around,
In this funland, happiness found!

Colors sparkle, twirl and twist,
In this realm, you can't resist.
Come join the fun, the tide won't stop,
In this briny world, we're on top!

Rhapsody of Marine Marvels

Crabs dance in their funky suits,
While starfish wear their silly boots.
Turtles twirl in a joyful spree,
Fish join in with glee, can't you see?

Seahorses floss, oh what a sight,
Blowing bubbles, floating light.
They gossip on a coral throne,
As clams chuckle in a silly tone.

Anemones wave their arms in cheer,
As dolphins dive without a fear.
They spin and splash, creating a show,
With laughter echoing below.

Bubbles burst and laughter flies,
As octopuses juggle, oh surprise!
The sea's a stage, and all are cast,
In this wacky world, fun's unsurpassed.

Currents of Enchantment

Shrimp in shades with sassy flair,
Flip and twist in salty air.
Clownfish giggle as they glide,
In underwater joy, they take pride.

Eels with wigs, what a dazzling scene,
Wobble and wiggle, looking so keen.
They tell jokes that make seaweed blush,
While jellyfish sway, all in a hush.

A pufferfish blows up, oh what a hoot,
Trying to scare a curious brute.
But the more they puff, the more they grin,
In this quirky show, who'll win?

Manta rays slide with graceful grace,
Doing the cha-cha in their space.
With every swirl and every flip,
They twist and turn, on a funny trip.

Echoing Riches of the Deep

Grouper in goggles makes quite a splash,
Dancing around with a youthful flash.
While barracudas play peek-a-boo,
In this pleasure dome, they've got a view.

Lobsters wear ties to formal affairs,
While clownfish crack wise without cares.
The sea's a place of whimsy and fun,
Where laughter ties everyone as one.

The anemone's prank on a snoozing fish,
Gives it a kiss, fulfills a wish.
A wiggly worm steals the spotlight too,
As crabs join in, then out of the blue!

The ocean's laughter flows like a stream,
With silly sights that make us beam.
Underwater, where joy comes alive,
It's a unique place where smiles thrive.

Fantasia of Flickering Fins

Fish wearing hats, a riotous sight,
Flipping and flopping in sheer delight.
Zip past shells, 'round coral bends,
In this fun world, the laughter never ends.

Plankton play peek, hide-and-seek's game,
Chasing each other, never the same.
In seaweed jungles where mischief reigns,
They bubble and giggle, escaping their chains.

Brine shrimp boogie, non-stop they groove,
Their funky moves making everyone move.
The ocean beats to a jazzy sound,
As everything dances, no one's left drowned.

So here's to the sea, its joy and its cheer,
Where silliness echoes, and laughter's near.
In coral caverns, the fun never stops,
As life bubbles over with giggles and pops.

Nautical Reverie at Dusk

As bubbles rise and fish do twirl,
A clownfish boasts of his bright pearl.
He tickles a turtle, makes him laugh,
In their watery world, they share a gaffe.

Starfish giggle, waving their arms,
While seahorses prance in their charming balms.
A jellyfish jives, doing a twist,
"Come join the party!" it scoffs, you get the gist!

An octopus jokingly hides in a sack,
Wearing a hat, just for the laugh track.
A sea urchin cracks jokes, quite absurd,
In this underwater realm, life is never blurred.

So ride the tides, let your heart be merry,
Dance with the waves, let worries be cherry.
In the twilight's shimmer, let friendships bloom,
As the ocean giggles, the currents consume.

Songs of the Shimmering Seafloor

The sea cucumber hums a funky tune,
While crabs tap dance under the light of the moon.
Their pincers clack, a symphony bright,
In this underwater hall, oh what a sight!

A shrimp plays drums on a clam shell tight,
While clownfish cheer, their colors so bright.
"I know a spot where the plankton flow,"
The wise old whale chants, with a wink, "let's go!"

Shrilling sea slugs sing in harmony,
While dolphins flip, oh so gracefully.
Each ripple a chorus, laughter like tides,
In this frolicsome world, each creature abides.

So guffaw with the grouper, twirl with the rays,
Each finned friend here has humorous ways.
In the shimmering depths, let joy strive,
For an ocean of giggles keeps dreams alive!

Ballad of the Ocean's Palette

In hues of blue, where the fishes dance,
A parrotfish grins, he's got quite the stance.
"Come try my colors, blue, green, and gold!"
He paints the waves with his stories bold.

A shy little puffer puts on a show,
He swells up so large, it gives quite a glow.
"Can you believe it? I'm buoyant and bright!"
With a laugh like bubbles, he floats with delight.

A starry ray performs tricks with grace,
While a naughty octopus paints its own face.
With spots and stripes, oh what a display,
In this whimsical world, colors won't fray.

So join the madness of the ocean spree,
Where laughter's the brush, and joy's the decree.
With every wave, let your spirit be free,
For life's a vibrant dance in the deep blue sea!

Chants of the Silent Swells

In the depths where the mermaids hum,
A whale belly laughs, sounding quite dumb.
"Why so serious?" he bubbles with glee,
In the depths of the calm, we're silly and free.

Anemones sway, with tickles they tease,
While schools of fish dart with effortless ease.
"Catch me if you can!" a guppy quips loud,
In this playful realm, find joy not a shroud.

A gentle sea breeze whispers sweet jokes,
While crabs pull pranks with their quirky pokes.
"Shell we dance?" a hermit asks in delight,
With laughter that echoes through day and night.

So listen closely to the ocean's delight,
Where fun is the current that carries us tight.
In the serene blue, let laughter unfurl,
For the heart of the sea is a whimsical whirl!

The Dance of Marine Life

In the ocean's grand parade,
Fish wear outfits, oh how they jade!
A clownfish jokes, while sharks just stare,
Octopuses twirl with stylish flair.

A seahorse bobbles, never in sync,
While turtles glide, they're such a wink!
With every splash, a giggle spreads,
As bubbles rise where laughter treads.

A crab does the tango, what a delight,
Prawns breakdance, oh what a sight!
Barnacles rock out, no need for a stage,
The sea's a dance floor, all fish engage!

So while the waves create their tune,
Fins and tails dance under the moon.
In this watery realm, joy's on display,
Where every finned friend loves to play!

Glistening Memories Under the Wave

In shallows bright, the memories gleam,
With starfish grins and a jellyfish beam.
The turtles laugh; they share old tales,
Of pirate ships with colorful sails.

A clam spills secrets from the sand,
While shrimps write novels with tiny hands.
The gossip spreads from one to the next,
About a lost sock—oh, what's the text?

Each scallop sways with a glittering grin,
Remembering times when the fun would begin.
Anemones poking, oh what a tease!
Making friends giggle with the gentle breeze.

So listen closely, among the corals bright,
You'll find sweet laughter that feels just right.
Among glistening memories etched in the tide,
These joyful whispers forever reside.

The Colorful Heartbeat of the Sea

With colors bright, the sea comes alive,
Each fish a star, together they thrive.
A grouper grins, while a trumpetfish plays,
Creating a spectacle that never decays.

Look at the parrotfish, rainbow in tow,
Its beak makes coral turn into a show.
Anemones chuckle in soft, wavy beats,
While sea cucumbers dance with their feets.

Oh, snap! A little pufferfish puffs,
While clownfish play tag, full of laughs and huffs.
The sea urchins roll their eyes with flair,
As eels weave tails through the salty air.

In this vibrant world where fun takes the lead,
Every aquatic friend has a story to read.
The heartbeat of waters, a vivid display,
In this carnival of joy, we happily sway!

A Chorus of Fish

Swim with the rhythm, a fishy delight,
A chorus erupts in the ocean's twilight.
With bubbles and splashes, a harmony grows,
As minnows compose with their fins in toes.

The angelfish giggles, its scales shining bright,
While blennies tell jokes, pure comedic fright.
A grouper leads sings with a bass so low,
While sardines form lines for the grand show.

Flipping and flopping, the guppies join in,
Creating a melody where giggles begin.
From deep to the shallow, their laughter resounds,
As sea stars clap, their joy knows no bounds.

In underwater rhythms, let's have a ball,
With fins and gills, we'll dance for them all.
The ocean a stage for this grand, fishy fight,
A chorus of laughter, all day and night!

The Chorus of the Blue

Fish in tuxedos dance with glee,
Waving their fins, oh what a spree!
Crabs in bow ties clicking to the beat,
A slippery party, quite the treat!

Starfish juggle shells with great flair,
Seahorses twirl without a care!
An octopus plays in fancy shoes,
Forget the blues, it's all good news!

Turtles glide like they own the floor,
While jellyfish float and softly snore!
This underwater bash is grand,
Who knew sea life's this well planned?

When the bubbles rise and laughter roars,
Fishy friends bustle through the doors!
With a splash, they sing, dance, and sway,
In this blue world, come join the play!

A Gathering of Marine Whispers

Clams gossip softly, shells all aflutter,
Tell tales of treasure, and the pearls they utter!
A dolphin chimes in with a cheeky grin,
"Did you see that shark? Now that's an amusing fin!"

Shrimps hold a conference, in secrecy deemed,
Plotting their movements, while seaweed dreamed.
With sea urchins guarding the secret delight,
"Why don't you all come and join us tonight?"

A playful otter slides in with style,
Wearing a smile that's quite worth the while.
"Who needs to hide? Let's all come out!"
In this coral crowd, we scream and shout!

As waves softly echo our light-hearted cheer,
In our underwater town, there's nothing to fear!
With laughter and shimmy, let's raise the toast,
For friendships and fun, we cherish the most!

Echoing Tales of the Ocean

Whale songs drift like bubblegum fluff,
"Have you heard tales? Oh, they're really tough!"
Anemones giggle, with giggles so bright,
While clownfish play tricks from morning till night!

Coral don hats, quite stylish indeed,
While snails slide by with enchanting speed.
"Yo ho ho! Look at my bling!"
Says the starfish, ready for the night to bring!

A parrotfish flexes his vibrant hues,
"Who needs the clouds? Down here, we choose!"
No pirate's treasure could match our gold,
These tales of the sea, they never get old!

In this ocean of whispers, laughter fish-tales,
Join us by moonlight, as humor prevails!
With salt in the air, and joy in our hearts,
We're all part of this big oceanic art!

Fable of the Coastal Waters

A crab in a cape struts by with pride,
While fish in sunglasses take a long glide.
"Did you see that whale? What a splash!"
The shoreline echoes with a humorous crash!

Sand dollars shimmer, exchanging their view,
"Dear starfish, tell me, what's new with you?"
"I've been on a diet," says one little ray,
"Still can't fit in, but I'm here to stay!"

Pelicans dive in for a casual meal,
While sea otters giggle, it's quite surreal!
"Oh look! There's a seal with a fishy friend!"
Their antics continue, it seems never to end!

So gather 'round waters, all creatures great and small,
Let's share in the laughter, it's fun for us all!
With shells and with tides, side by side we'll sing,
In this coastal fable, joy's the real king!

The Undersea Chorus

In the depths, fish do a dance,
With bubbles and giggles, they'll entrance.
A crab's doing the cha-cha with flair,
While seahorses twirl without a care.

Starfish flip in their own great style,
And clams start to clap, just for a while.
The octopus juggles with eight wiggly arms,
While dolphins play tag with their silly charms.

The seaweed sways to the music's beat,
Anemones groove on their minnow fleet.
Whales sing the tunes, oh what a sight,
As anglerfish laugh, glowing in the night.

Grouper and snapper join in the fun,
While plankton turn flips just to stun.
In this underwater fun-filled spree,
There's laughter, and joy, oh what glee!

Luminous Sonatas of the Abyss

In the dark, there's a glow, what a delight,
With jellyfish dancing in the pale moonlight.
A squid holds a concert, ink in the air,
The seahorse stands up, it's a fanciful fair.

Turtles are twirling, acting so spry,
While clownfish giggle, swimming nearby.
A symphony plays on coral all day,
As shrimp play the drums in their unique way.

An orchestra fishes, scales shining bright,
The starry night hides creatures in flight.
A chorus of bubbles rises above,
As conch shells echo the sea's gentle love.

With each finished tune, they laugh and they play,
In this watery world where they all sway.
Under the surface, the melodies flow,
In the grand show of nature, come watch the glow!

Currents of Wonder

Amidst the currents, fish dart and dive,
With each little movement, they're so alive.
A pufferfish giggles, puffing with pride,
While clownfish swim by, they just can't hide.

A sponge hosts a party, all friends will attend,
With shrimp on the menu, let's not pretend!
The sea cucumbers play limbo with style,
As eels weave around with a sparkling smile.

Coral formations create a grand stage,
Where shrimp and their pals act out their age.
The seafoam laughs with each wild twist,
While fish form a line, it's an oceanic tryst.

In swirling waters, the jokes go along,
With laughter and splashes, we sing our song.
Join in the fun, as we kick up the sand,
In currents of wonder, take my hand!

Whirling Wonders of the Sea

In the swirling tide, a clam starts to spin,
With a wink and a nod, it's a quirky win.
Turtles are twirling, swirling so free,
While snappy little fishes giggle with glee.

The sea snails move in an elegant race,
As jellyfish float, they give chase with grace.
Starfish form bands with their five-legged jam,
While a dolphin pops up, 'Hey, look at me, Pam!'

The waves bring a waltz, the seaweed sways,
As crabs crab-shuffle, oh what a craze!
A lighthouse beams down, casting its light,
While fish troop together, a wonderful sight.

With clam shells clapping, the ocean doth sing,
In this whirling wonder, let your heart swing.
Dive into the laughter, join in the play,
In the whirling wonders where we splash all day!

Soundtrack of the Bristle Star's Voyage

In the deep, the fish all dance,
With bristle stars in a funny prance.
They wiggle and jiggle, it's quite a sight,
Underwater disco, oh what a night!

Shrimp play trumpets, crabs keep time,
Each bubble pops to the beat of a rhyme.
Octopuses tap with colorful flair,
While jellyfish float, light as air.

The seaweed sways like a party hat,
Anemones giggle, 'Is that a catfish spat?'
As the currents swirl, making a fuss,
Even the starfish join in, what a plus!

From the depths to the surface, the laughter spreads,
With all of their friends, nobody treads.
When the tide winks, they all sing loud,
A symphony of silliness, so proud!

Tides of Life's Canvas

In a vibrant world where colors bloom,
Wave after wave, they chase the moon.
Fish with glasses say, 'Is that a snack?'
While snails on rocks laugh, 'Hey, watch your back!'

Paintbrushes of coral brush the sea,
The canvas of life, a sight to see.
Seahorses waltz in their tiny shoes,
While clams clap shells, breaking the blues.

The starfish pose, each one a star,
Strutting their stuff, saying 'Look at us, far!'
With bubbles of laughter floating around,
Their art of joy knows no bound.

Every tide brings a new quirky scene,
With laughter and colors, forever serene.
Dive in and enjoy this playful show,
Where the tides of life happily flow!

Colorful Reflections in Liquid Light

Beneath the waves where colors clash,
Fish in tuxedos create quite a splash.
Rainbow trout whisper, 'What's the fuss?'
While clownfish chuckle, 'We're all in one bus!'

"Who's the best dressed?" they giggle and croon,
As they swim round the reefs, singing their tune.
Bubble-blowers pufferfish puff up with pride,
While sea cucumbers slide by, fun to ride.

The seaweed twirls in a dress of green,
As the hermit crabs boast of the shells they've seen.
Turtles snicker, 'Are those fins or flippers?'
Every fin-tastic dance gets the heart to quippers!

As sunlight dances through layers of blue,
The fish sing out, 'Hey, come join the crew!'
In this vibrant world, laughter takes flight,
With colorful reflections, pure delight!

Dreams Born of Aquatic Harmony

Ocean dreams, a whimsical spree,
In the water, it's a jubilee!
Dancing dolphins in a conga line,
With sea urchins grinning, feeling divine.

Every wave tells a playful tale,
As turtles groove with a jazzy wail.
Scatter of fish, like confetti, they dart,
Stingrays slide by, wearing stealthy art.

Pillow of sand, a soft place to rest,
Where clams tell jokes and all feel blessed.
"Knock knock," says the crab, "Who's there, you see?"
"Just me and my shell, come dance by the sea!"

In this harmony where giggles thrive,
Every creature knows how to jive.
With dreams of laughter that never fade,
Together beneath the waves, fun is made!

The Artistry of the Tide

A crab in a bowtie, quite dapper and spry,
Struts to the beat, like a funk band nearby.
Fish in their sequins, they twirl and they dive,
Making their splash, oh, they feel so alive!

Turtles in shades, drifting by with a grin,
Gossiping jellyfish, let the gossip begin!
With laughter that bubbles, the seaweed does sway,
As tempests of giggles fill up the bay!

When plankton throw parties, it's quite a surprise,
The kraken shows up, in disguise with his fries.
They dance on the surfaces, up and then down,
Making waves of their joy, across the blue town!

So next time you gaze at the sea's joyful throng,
Remember it's nature that hums the best song.
For under the surface, it's magic and glee,
In the waters where bubbles and laughter roam free!

Swirls of Life and Laughter

Bubbles that giggle, while fish paint the scene,
Pinching sea cucumbers with tickles between.
Octopuses juggling, their balls all afloat,
'Look ma,' they wave, 'we're on a fun boat!'

Starfish in a conga line, moving with flair,
Shrimp with tiny hats, dance light as air.
The sea anemones, with their hairstyles divine,
Snicker at stony corals, 'Hey, life's so fine!'

A dolphin with swagger, clicks jokes on the side,
His friends all around him, laughter amplified.
As waves rise to brush every creature around,
Nature's grand theater, full of joy, so profound!

In the ocean's embrace, where silliness thrives,
Remember to smile, for this is where life jives.
Amongst all the ripples, let happiness flow,
In this swirl of delight, where all creatures know!

Mosaic of the Ocean Floor

A mosaic of colors, like paint on a wall,
Clams tap their shells, hold a sharp morning call.
These creatures with quirks, all merry and bright,
In the orchestra of water, fun dances in light!

Peeking from their reef homes, the snails roll their eyes,
"Did you see that dolphin? He thinks he's so wise!"
With shrimp in a ruckus, they wiggle and play,
Fighting for the spotlight, in the sun's golden ray!

Schooling fish giggle, as they swirl left and right,
Simulating whirlwinds with ridiculous might.
Anemones waving, with arms oh so wide,
Make way for this party; let's all take a ride!

So surrender your worries, dive deep with a cheer,
The ocean's a canvas; life's jokes bring good beer.
For as long as it dances, and laughter survives,
We celebrate beauty—the fun that derives!

Spirals of Life Beneath the Sea

There's a whirl of laughter in the deep, cool blue,
Where critters wear costumes, oh, the fun they pursue!
Giant squids in top hats, feeling so swell,
With each graceful swirl, they consume the sea shell!

Bubble-eyed fish, they giggle with glee,
A clam tells a story, oh wait, a tall sea!
Corals like grandmothers, knitting with pride,
'Is it a canapé? Or maybe a tide?'

Seahorses prance, like they're out on the town,
Wiggling their tails, never wearing a frown.
Starfish join in, they wiggle their legs,
While laughter erupts, it's like dancing with dregs!

So next time you wander, in oceans so wide,
Join in on the fun, let your giggles collide.
For under the waves, where the silly fish dart,
Life's joy is a treasure, it's nature's own art!

Harmony of Coral Dreams

In the sea with colors bright,
Fish in bow ties dance with delight.
Octopus plays with a paintbrush flair,
Creating art that floats through the air.

Clams clap along with a rhythmic thud,
Sea stars twirl in a glittery flood.
Turtles wiggle, trying to steal the show,
While seaweed giggles, swaying to and fro.

Bubbles pop like confetti delight,
As shrimp wear hats that shimmer in light.
Jellyfish float in a jelly parade,
Every creature joins in, unafraid.

In this underwater fiesta so grand,
Every fin and tail makes a funky band.
With laughter of waves, the ocean does beam,
In this whimsical world, we all chase our dream.

Ballad of Underwater Realms

In blue waters where laughter thrives,
A crab in shades does the hokey survive.
Grouper performs a surprising flip,
While the clowns throw bubbles, taking a dip.

Eels in bow ties swim with great class,
While sea horses prance, oh what a sass!
Dolphins play tag, giggling through the space,
In this underwater race, joy wears a face.

Clownfish juggle with pebbles and seaweed,
In this coastal carnival, laughter's a creed.
Anemones applaud with their soft, swaying arms,
Each fin and finning skill brings a warmth and charms.

A mermaid sings as she twirls on her stone,
Making every fish feel right at home.
Together they dance, in a splashy embrace,
In this merry stream, laughter takes place.

Lullaby of the Ocean Floor

At twilight deep where silliness drapes,
An anglerfish shines and giggles with shapes.
Starfish on stage, they kick to the beat,
While crabs do the cha-cha with pinching feet.

Seahorses conjure new spells of delight,
Bubbling up laughter, without any fright.
A conch shell hums out a melodious tune,
As fish dance together, all under the moon.

Coral blooms twirl in their colorful gear,
While sea cucumbers slide down with cheer.
The anemone sways, waving high and low,
Join the coral cabaret, steal the show!

As night drapes the ocean, the fun won't pause,
Tidal waves whisper gentle applause.
Each bubble that rises sings sweetly of dreams,
In this ocean lullaby, joy streams.

Starlit Patterns in the Blue

Under starlit waves, where funny things roam,
A lobster's using a fork as a comb.
Nemo's got jokes that are truly bizarre,
While blowfish laugh, puffing up in their car.

Dancing with seaweed, an orange clown prances,
While starfish groove, taking silly chances.
Barnacles giggle as they stick to the ground,
Creating a band with a rustling sound.

With a dolphin's flip and a jellyfish sway,
Ocean critters sing a bright, joyous play.
Turtles join in with a shell-shaking twist,
In this underwater party, none can resist.

So dive into fun, let the waters take flight,
Where the laughter rings deep through day and through night.
With every bubble that bursts in the sea,
The ocean's a canvas, so let it be free!

Shifting Sands and Singing Corals

On sandy shores where crabs do dance,
A clam once wore a bright pink pants.
The seaweed sways, it bends with glee,
Claiming it's a rockstar, wild and free.

The jellyfish are quite a sight,
With disco moves that last all night.
They shimmy, shake, and take the lead,
In the underwater party, oh indeed!

A starfish tries to tell a joke,
But it's just a "star" that's rather broke.
It laughs at every pun and jest,
While sea cucumbers, they just rest.

A turtle joins with a silly grin,
Says, "Slow and steady? That's just a win!"
With seaweed wigs and bubble hats,
They throw a bash for all the cats.

Luminescence of the Silent Deep

In waters deep where silence reigns,
Glowfish twinkle like window panes.
With luminescent flare they boast,
Turning night into a glowing coast.

An octopus in polka dots,
Dances in circles, ties itself in knots.
It flashes colors, a grand display,
"Look at me!" it shouts, "I'm here to play!"

The anglerfish grins from afar,
With a lighted lure, a real bizarre.
"Come closer, friends!" it gleefully calls,
But the others just giggle, and swim past the walls.

"Bubbles!" squeaks a shrimp in delight,
As it blows them big, a hilarious sight.
With every pop, a chuckle erupts,
In the silent deep, laughter interrupts.

Dreamcatchers of the Sea

Beneath the waves where dreams take flight,
A seahorse rides into the night.
It catches dreams in tangled weeds,
Hopes and wishes, along with deeds.

"Hold on tight!" a dolphin squeaks,
Jumping through light, oh how it peaks.
"Watch me soar, I'm swift and spry,
Like a kite that kisses the sky!"

A pufferfish feels quite the thrill,
Puffing up, it shows its skill.
"It's not just size, but style you see,
I'm a fashionista, that's really me!"

The bottom dwellers make a fuss,
Painting shells while others rush.
"Create a dream, a catchy tune,
Underwater disco, let's all buffoon!"

Singing Stones of the Ocean

Along the shore where stones do sing,
A rock once claimed a crown, a king.
It hummed a tune that made waves sway,
While barnacles danced, all night and day.

A pebble chuckled, "Is it just me?
Or do these waves hold a symphony?"
With every splash, a new verse formed,
Making rhythms that were truly warmed.

Seagulls squawk and join the band,
With silly solos, they make their stand.
"Let's harmonize!" a clam declares,
As mussels chime in with songs of cares.

A conch gets ready, takes a breath,
"This solo's mine; I'll aim for the best!"
And with a blast, it sounds the alarm,
The ocean's laughter, its greatest charm.

The Language of Sea Frolic

In the ocean, fish do dance,
With bubbles making quite a prance.
A crab in a tux, quite the sight,
As jellyfish float, day turns to night.

Seahorses gossip, tails entwined,
While clowns in big shoes, humor aligned.
A dolphin tricks a thinking ray,
As octopuses paint the day.

Mermaids giggle, tails a-swish,
Playing hide-and-seek with a fish.
Turtles, they spin, show off their shells,
With seaweed wigs, they sing their spells.

In this realm of water and fun,
Every critter seeks a pun.
With laughter echoing through the tide,
Sea creatures party, side by side.

Celestial Dreams in the Tides

Starfish waltz, what a funny sight,
Under the moon, gleaming so bright.
Anemones giggle, tickling the sand,
While clams crustaceans hold hands.

Seashells whisper tales of old,
Of fish that wore stories, bold and gold.
Crabs don shades, look so refined,
Stirring in waters, humor intertwined.

A pelican dives, splashing with flair,
Laughing at fish that dart in despair.
With a squawk and a flap, he calls,
While sea turtles line up for beach balls.

In these celestial tides, they scheme,
With dreams of laughter, life's a dream.
The ocean sings of joy and fun,
Where every wave is a joke well spun.

Murmurs of the Deep Blue

Whales whistle, deep and low,
While anglerfish start the show.
A parrotfish sings, munching a leaf,
Jokes hide in coral, beyond belief.

Sandy bottoms giggle wide,
As minnows join the playful ride.
Squids in ink play hide and seek,
While turtles give a cheeky peek.

The sea cucumbers share some laughs,
With quirks in their squishy paths.
Clownfish chuckle, tails a-wag,
At seaweed humor, all in a brag.

In the depths, where laughter flows,
Each creature knows how fun it goes.
With bubbles tickling the waves above,
Murmurs of joy, the ocean's love.

Figures in a Watercolor World

In a world of colors, bright and fair,
Tropical fish dye the salty air.
A starfish in polka dots takes a stroll,
Painting smiles on turtles, making them whole.

Watercolors splash with every turn,
As seagulls squawk, it's their turn to learn.
With each brushstroke, stories unfurl,
From the giggling waves to the twirling whirl.

Coral castles hold court today,
While octopuses dance in a quirky ballet.
Each sea creature a work of art,
With laughter painted on every heart.

In this watercolor world so free,
Joy swims alongside the fish, you see.
Creating a canvas, mutual fun,
Where the sea's laughter is never done.

Waves of Colorful Harmony

In a sea of flip-flops, fish do cha-cha,
Dancing on waves like a quirky brava.
Octopuses juggle, tossing shells here and there,
Oh, the fun they have, without a single care!

Crabs in their taxis, racing for fun,
Cracking up jokes under the warm sun.
The clownfish giggle, making peachy faces,
Tickling each seaweed as laughter embraces!

Starfish are dreaming, counting the tides,
While seahorses twirl in their stylish rides.
Oh, what a party, a bubble-filled show,
In this underwater, goofy, vibrant glow!

So come take a dive, join the laughter parade,
In the wacky sea where magic is made.
With colors colliding, the fun's never done,
Together we splash, oh, isn't this fun?

The Symphony of Shadows and Light

Bubbles rising up, they tickle the fish,
Creating a tune with every quick swish.
Turtles are crooning, in their slow serenade,
While sea cucumbers join, feeling so brave!

A band of shrimps plays on tiny guitars,
While eels wrap around, doing dance with the stars.
Jellyfish glowing, floating like dreams,
Composing sweet nonsense through shimmering beams.

Clownfish are joking, with laughter they twine,
Testing their puns on the sea turtle line.
Caught in a whirlpool of bubbles and rays,
They spin through the waters, a zany ballet!

In shadows they shuffle, in light they delight,
An oceanic symphony, what a grand sight!
Bring on the fun, in this watery spree,
Where shadows and music create harmony!

Coral's Secret Language

Among polka-dot corals, secrets abound,
Whispers of wiggly worms all around.
In this chatty paradise, gossips parade,
Squid share their tales while playing charades!

A sea turtle winks, saying 'What's the news?',
Fish swap their colors, buzzing like a fuse.
Lobsters have stories etched deep in their shells,
While sea urchins giggle, holding their spells.

The sea anemones wiggle with glee,
Telling tall tales like a fancy degree.
With bubbles and giggles, they're making a scene,
In coral's vast palace where laughter is keen!

So bring your bright ears, let the chatter unfold,
In coral's sweet language, let the fun be bold.
Dive into the chatter where giggles reflect,
In this undersea world we all can connect!

Seashell Gospels

Shells tell their stories, oh listen, my friend,
Of waves that have tickled every sandy bend.
With whispers of sailors and mermaids in tow,
Their secrets are treasures from long, long ago!

Snails play their horns, in a rascal parade,
A soft symphony made from the beach's cascade.
Puffers blow bubbles like giggles from the deep,
While sand dollars wink in their private keep.

Every sea feather carries a whimsy tale,
As crabs share their gossip from the mud-dwelling trail.
Clams are in chorus, with a click and a clack,
Dancing in rhythm, never looking back!

So grab your own shell and join in the fun,
A giddy galore as the sea tides run!
The gospels of shells hold the laughter of seas,
With echoes of joy riding each playful breeze!

Harmony of Colors Lost

In the ocean's bright embrace,
A clownfish lost his way,
He swam past jelly's dance,
And thought it was ballet.

He giggled with a seahorse,
Who wore a dazzling tie,
Together they would twirl,
And play beneath the sky.

But when a turtle cheered,
With laughter mighty loud,
They bumped right into corals,
And startled all the crowd.

Then all the fish just chuckled,
At this grand, silly show,
In the colors of the reef,
Where friendship seems to flow.

Serenade of the Sea's Garden

In a garden made of waves,
A lobster wrote a tune,
He played on shells of fish,
Beneath a happy moon.

A starfish sang along,
With six arms in the air,
While clamsbeat times together,
They filled the ocean air.

The octopus brought snacks,
With eight limbs stacking chips,
They shared their joyful feast,
With laughs that made them flip.

These tunes echoed in bubbles,
Around the coral's bend,
In this garden full of giggles,
Where every sea friend blends.

Echoes from the Tidal Abyss

Down where the murky shadows live,
A fish tried to take a nap,
But under the waves, what a ruckus!
A squid drew on a map.

He claimed he found Atlantis,
With treasure by the ton,
But it turned out a sea sponge,
Was hiding and just spun.

The echoes danced around,
With laughter through the tide,
As all the creatures joined,
In this watery joyride.

With bubbles full of giggles,
And seaweed swaying strong,
In the depths of endless fun,
Was the ocean's silly song.

Dance of the Vibrant Polyps

Tiny polyps sway and whirl,
In colors bright and bold,
They throw a disco party,
Wearing costumes made of gold.

A crab brought all his buddies,
In hats both strange and neat,
They danced beneath the moonlight,
With six tiny dancing feet.

A shrimp forgot his rhythm,
And slipped upon a shell,
His fellow friends just laughed and cheered,
As he began to yell.

But in this vibrant underwater,
With polyp moves so right,
They spun and twirled in laughter,
Till dawn kissed off the night.

Breath of the Marine Kingdom

Bubbles rise and fish do twirl,
A wriggly dance in a watery swirl.
Seahorses giggle, clownfish grin,
With every splash, the fun begins!

Turtles glide, they don't look back,
While snails race down a salty track.
Octopuses play hide and seek,
With ink so blue, they peek and squeak!

A crab with bling struts by the reef,
Calling all to join his beef.
With a sideways shuffle and a cheer,
He waves a claw and brings the beer!

With every wave, laughter flows,
In this kingdom where joy glows.
So take a dive and join the fun,
Under the waves, we're never done!

Dance of the Vibrant Waters

In currents quick, the fishes flip,
Their colorful gowns make quite the trip.
Dancing starfish in a conga line,
Wiggle and giggle, feel so fine!

Anemones sway like they're at a ball,
Jellyfish twirl with no care at all.
Waves crash in with a big splash sound,
While sea turtles bust a move all around!

A clam joins in with a maracas shake,
While dolphins jump for a big belly flake.
Everyone's laughing, oh what a sight,
In waters where fun takes flight!

So plunge right in and be a part,
Of this joyful dance that warms the heart.
With fins or feet, it doesn't matter,
Let joy bubble up, and laughter scatter!

Serenade of the Hidden Depths

From coral crannies, a tune comes through,
A tuba played by a snapper or two.
Clownfish hum in a comical key,
While parrotfish croon, "Come sing with me!"

Shells start clapping like they're at a show,
With sea cucumbers joining the flow.
The eel plays guitar, a slippery strum,
As all underwater begin to hum!

A puffer fish puffs with a silly face,
Trying to keep up with the bass line's pace.
Their rhythm goes wild beneath the sea blue,
Creating a concert that's just for you!

So come take a seat in this oceanic spot,
Where laughter and music dance quite a lot.
In the embrace of the waves, don't be shy,
Join in the serenade – let your spirit fly!

Rhythms of the Aquatic Garden

In gardens deep where laughter blooms,
A merry chorus spins out of rooms.
With fish that jiggle and crabs that crawl,
The ocean's party is a ball for all!

Green seaweed sways to a funky beat,
While squids squirt ink in a playful feat.
Starfish shine under a disco light,
As the whole ocean celebrates the night!

A rock anemone does a spin,
A dance that brings everyone in.
With sea urchins bouncing and shells in tow,
The rhythm of fun continues to flow!

So gather 'round in this garden so bright,
Where laughter bubble-lamps illuminate the night.
With every splash, a new friend to meet,
Let the aquatic rhythms get you on your feet!

www.ingramcontent.com/pod-product-compliance
Lightning Source LLC
Chambersburg PA
CBHW072217070526
44585CB00015B/1383